What is happening to me?

What do I do?

A Girls Guide

By María Báez

Illustrated By Troy Palmer-Hughes

Note:

Girls, to be friendlier and
have fun in this guide
I have called menstruation
"Red Dot", so be aware!

What is happening to me?
What do I do?
A Girls Guide

First Edition

Copyright © 2010 María Báez

ISBN: 978-1456489427

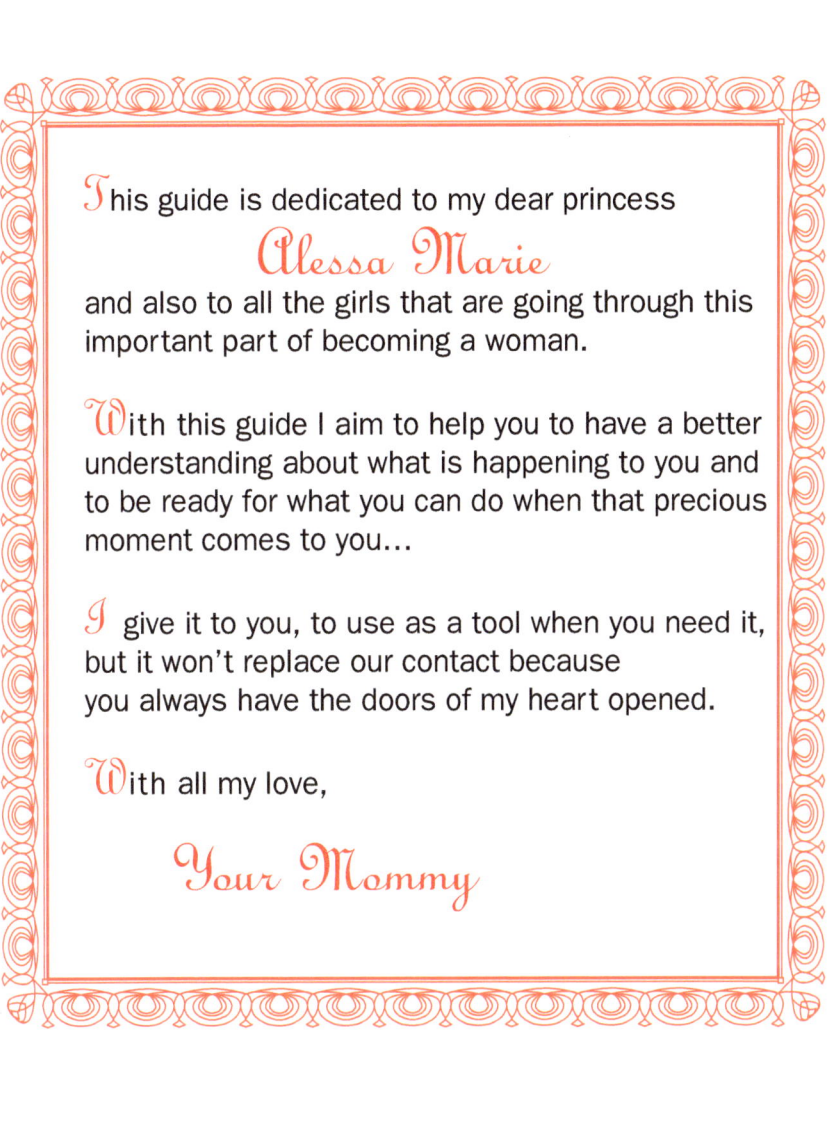

This guide is dedicated to my dear princess
Alessa Marie
and also to all the girls that are going through this
important part of becoming a woman.

With this guide I aim to help you to have a better
understanding about what is happening to you and
to be ready for what you can do when that precious
moment comes to you…

I give it to you, to use as a tool when you need it,
but it won't replace our contact because
you always have the doors of my heart opened.

With all my love,

Your Mommy

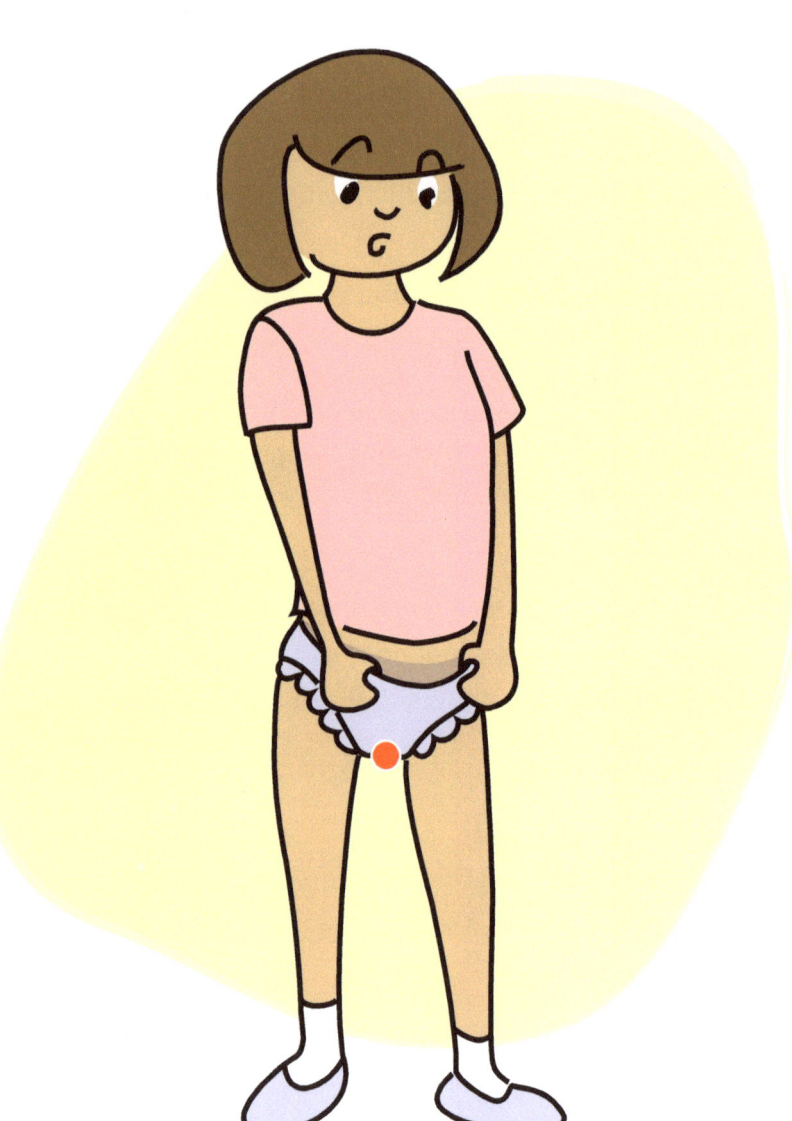

What is happening to me?

There is something physiological happening in your body, nothing is wrong with you. It happens to almost all women each month and is called menstruation.

You will notice the moment you see a certain amount of yellowish fluid, including blood, through the vagina.

Don't panic! Red Dot is not something bad happening to you, it is a sign that your body is normal, healthy and is preparing for adulthood. It means a child is becoming a big girl, then a woman.

Each period is part of the natural cycle called the menstrual cycle. This happens in a girl's body when it's time to develop your reproductive system.

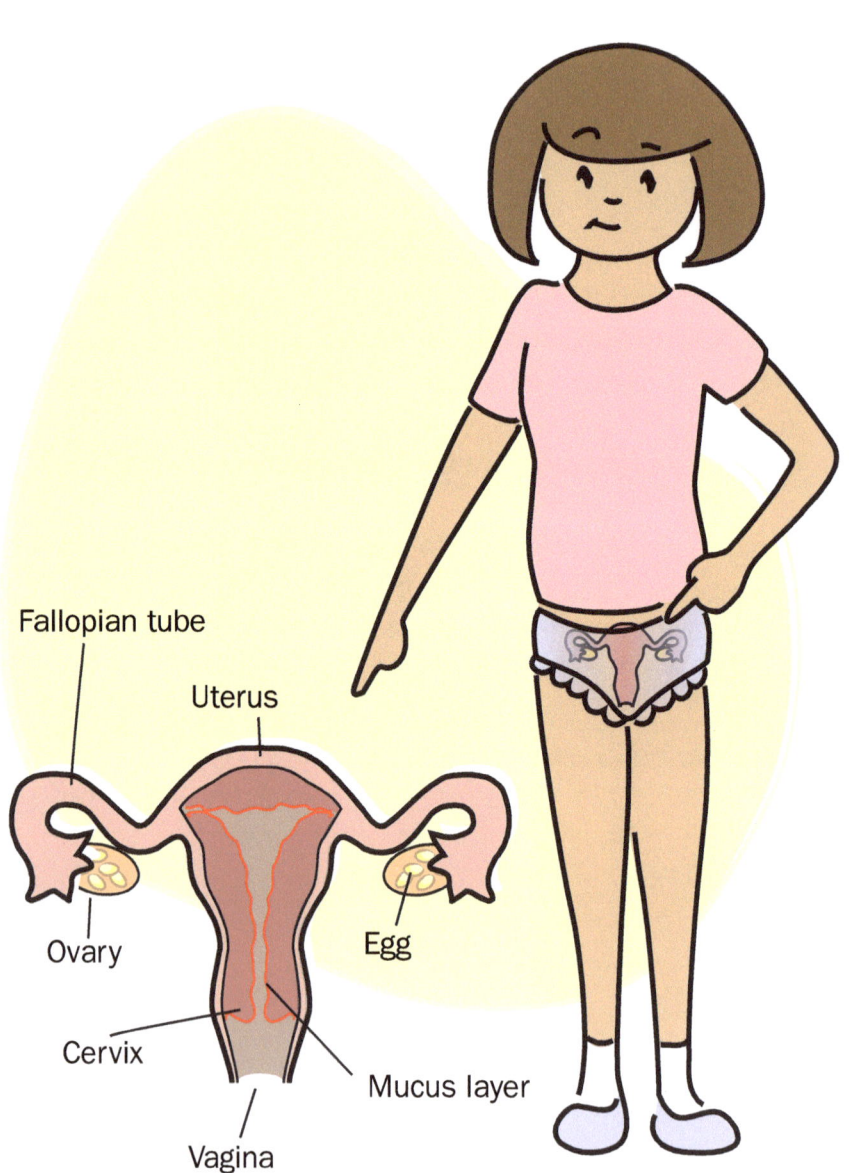

Fallopian tube

Uterus

Ovary

Egg

Cervix

Mucus layer

Vagina

In which part of my body does the menstrual cycle happen?

The menstrual cycle happens in the female reproductive system that has the following organs: the ovaries (which contain eggs), fallopian tubes, uterus and vagina.

What happens inside my body?

Your reproductive system goes through a phase in which the sex hormones of your body starts what is called ovulation. An egg is expelled from inside of the ovary into the fallopian tubes. When there is no fertilization of the egg, the mucus layer inside the uterus breaks down, breaking some capillaries, causing bleeding from the vagina.

When will I get the Red Dot?

There is no "accurate" time that your Red Dot will start; it will be when your body is ready. Most girls usually have their first Red Dot between 10 and 16 years old, average age is 12 years, although there have been cases where it comes at 8 years old (rarely).

Will I lose a lot of blood?

Don't panic! The amount of blood that is normally lost in the Red Dot is usually between 80 and 85 milliliters, more or less like 1/3 cup. Of this amount approximately 35 milliliters (about 5 tablespoons) is blood and the rest is vaginal discharge. It may seem a lot, but, in reality it is not. Your body contains more than 3,500 milliliters (about 20 cups) of blood.

How long will it last?

Between 3 and 7 days. Almost all girls have their Red Dot every month, because the time between the first day of her Red Dot and the next is 28 days, although some may be less and other more. Either way, if you're between 21 and 35 days, it is normal.

Tips!

After the first Red Dot, it would be good to use a calendar and note when each Red Dot begins and when it ends...

This will help you be prepared for each cycle and is the best way to know what is normal for you.

What are the signs of the Red Dot?

As I told you, everything will depend on your own development and growth of body, but you must be alert when you see changes in your body such as your breasts begin to grow, pubic hair appears and under arm hair, occurrence of vaginal discharge etc...

Tips! When you begin to menstruate, it is possible that your periods are not very regular. For example, it may be two or three months between Red Dots, or every Red Dot may last 1 day or 10 days. Do not worry, this is normal, your body will take time to establish regular menstrual cycles, which may take up to two years.

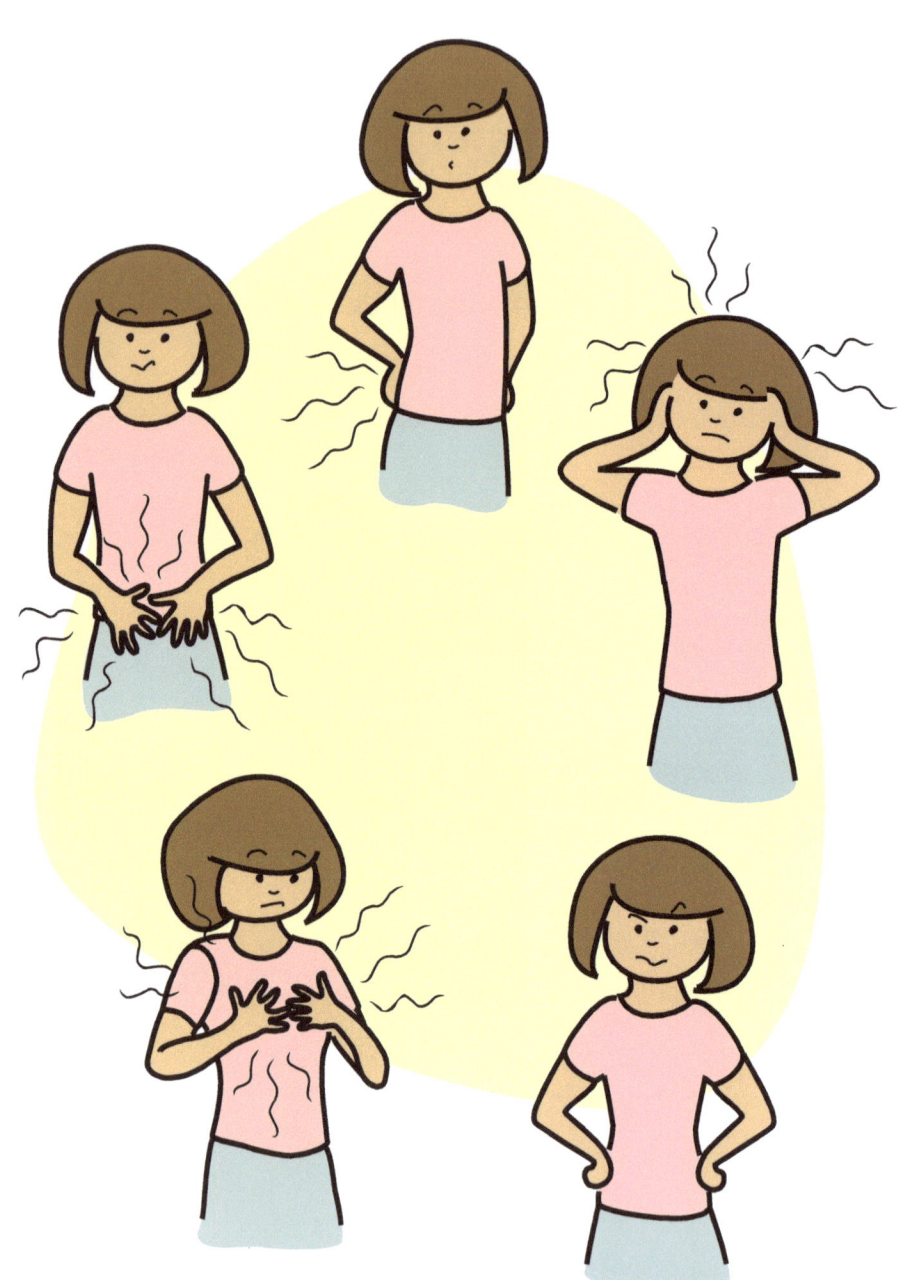

Will it hurt?

Not necessarily. Some girls only feel pain occasionally and some never do. But I must warn that you can feel symptoms ranging from cramping in the lower abdomen, back pain, headaches, etc. This is because the uterus is contracting to help eliminate most of its interior. If you have these symptoms or other discomfort during your Red Dot , do not be alarmed because they usually end the first or second day. There are also ways to alleviate them, for example: exercise, good nutrition, getting enough sleep etc...

Do breasts ache before the Red Dot?

You may feel discomfort or swelling and pain that are caused by the change in hormone levels. This is because of some fluid buildup in your breasts that makes them more sensitive and heavy. Do not worry, this feeling will pass quickly once your Red Dot has ended.

Will I go through emotional changes these days?

Yes, usually you are more sensitive and you may feel tired and heavy. Before your Red Dot your body stores more water than normal, which can make you feel bloated. It is also normal to feel a bit uncomfortable during puberty, this is because you are growing and changing very rapidly.

How can I relieve the pain?

The first thing to do that makes you feel better, is relaxing by giving yourself a warm bath, place a "heating pad" or something warm on your tummy, or do a little gentle exercise, etc.

Tips!!!

If pain is severe, there are good analgesics at the pharmacy. Be careful with the choice and ask mammy first, because these drugs should be evaluated by a health care provider or your doctor.

What do I do if my first Red Dot happens to me at school?

In general, all the girls are taken by surprise their first Red Dot, so do not worry, but get ready! It's always a good idea to carry in your schoolbag a smaller bag packed with a pad and clean underwear, just in case. If you forgot that day and do not have a pad available, you can use a bit of rolled toilet paper or tissues. Ask a school teacher to help you; it will not bother anyone to tell you what to do. Many schools have some pads available to help cases like this.

Will others realize when I have my Red Dot?

No! Unless you say it ... Nobody will notice!

Will I produce any odor when I have my Red Dot?

You can produce odor because the menstrual flow causes the odor when in contact with air.

Tips!!!

The best thing you can do against smelly is to change your pad every 3-4 hours and try to wash regularly.

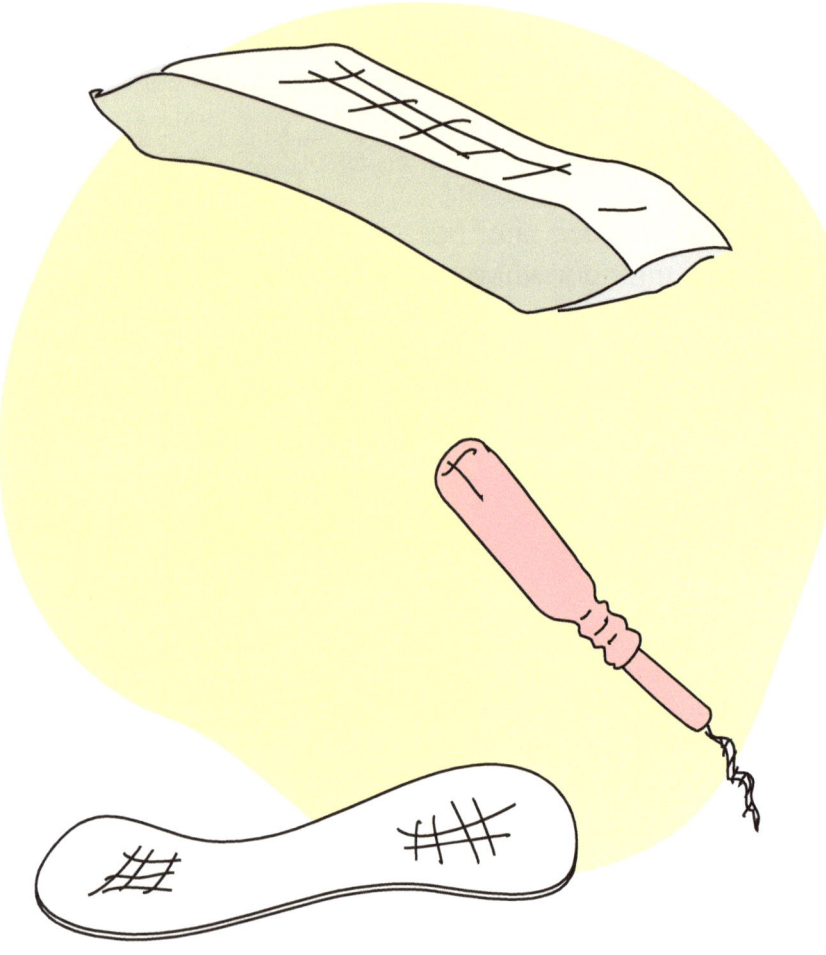

What do I have to use for those days?

Today there are many brands and different types of sanitary pads and tampons used to absorb menstrual flow when it is removed from your body. The pads attach to your underwear and absorb the menstrual flow after exiting the vagina. There is no absolute rule if you use thick or thin pads. It's preferable to use ultra thin because they are made of a special material that is super absorbent, which means that moisture is trapped inside and cannot come out. The super thin pads are comfortable and unobtrusive, while providing excellent protection and you feel clean and dry. Remember, it is important to change the pads several times a day. Another method is Tampons, which absorb the flow from inside the vagina as it exits the womb.

Tips!!!

Before using any method it's always good to talk with mom or your guardian to determinate the best for you, and consult your doctor. Use what you feel most comfortable. All systems are equally safe.

Is there something that I cannot do while having my Red Dot?

No. Your daily life and activities must be just as usual. Having Red Dot is not being sick, but rather you see it as a healthy and normal part of being female. With the menstrual period you can go to school, help with home work, see your friends, and play sports, swim at the beach or pool, or whatever you want.

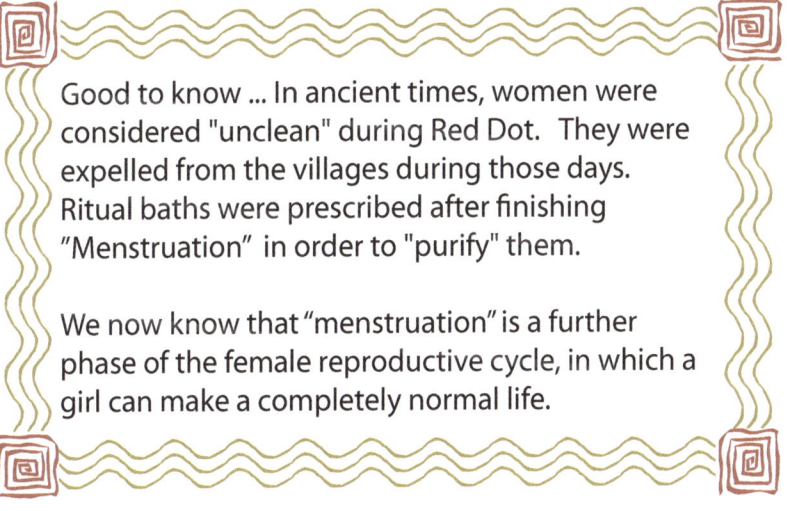

Good to know ... In ancient times, women were considered "unclean" during Red Dot. They were expelled from the villages during those days. Ritual baths were prescribed after finishing "Menstruation" in order to "purify" them.

We now know that "menstruation" is a further phase of the female reproductive cycle, in which a girl can make a completely normal life.

Who do I talk to when I get my Red Dot?

When that time comes do not feel embarrassed to talk about it with Mom, remember that Mommy also has a period every month. She knows exactly what to do and how to help.

$\mathcal{I}$ hope you now have a better idea of what "Red Dot" means, but if you didn't understand at the first reading, please don't get frustrated because as you're going through this you will comprehend… it happened to me too!

$\mathcal{A}$nd keep in mind, Red Dot is a natural and wonderful part of being a woman, because otherwise you wouldn't be here.

$\mathcal{I}$n the next page I will give you some descriptions that I mentioned in this guide with the intention of becoming more familiar with this topic. You can keep this guide as a reference in your pocket every time you have a question.

$\mathcal{R}$emember, always ask!

Descriptions

Sperm: is a cell that is part of the male reproductive organ. Its function is the formation of a new being when merging with the egg from the woman's reproductive system.

Egg: embryo, egg, zygote, embryo, macrogamete.

Fallopian tube: each of the tubes that connect with the ovaries.

Ovulation: the natural shedding of an egg from the ovary so it can go its way and be fertilized.

Fertilize: joining the male and female reproductive elements to give rise to a new being.

Fertilization of an egg: if the path of the egg in the fallopian tube encounters some "sperm", this egg is fertilized. It continues its journey, reaching the wall of the uterus and stays there, which would lead to the formation of a baby.

Physiological: organic, vital, functional somatic.

Sex hormones: product of the secretion of certain glands in the body of animals and plants, transported by the blood or sap. Regulates the activity of other organs.

Testosterone: is a male sex hormone.

Menopause: natural cessation of menstrual cycle in women. Women are fertile until menopause.

Buffers: Roll cotton, cellulose or other material that is inserted into the vagina to absorb menstrual flow.

www.ingramcontent.com/pod-product-compliance
Lightning Source LLC
Chambersburg PA
CBHW040327010626